DO-IT-YOURSELF STRATEGIC PLANNING

by: BILL TREASURER, FOUNDER, GIANT LEAP CONSULTING, INC.

LITTLE LEAPS
PRESS

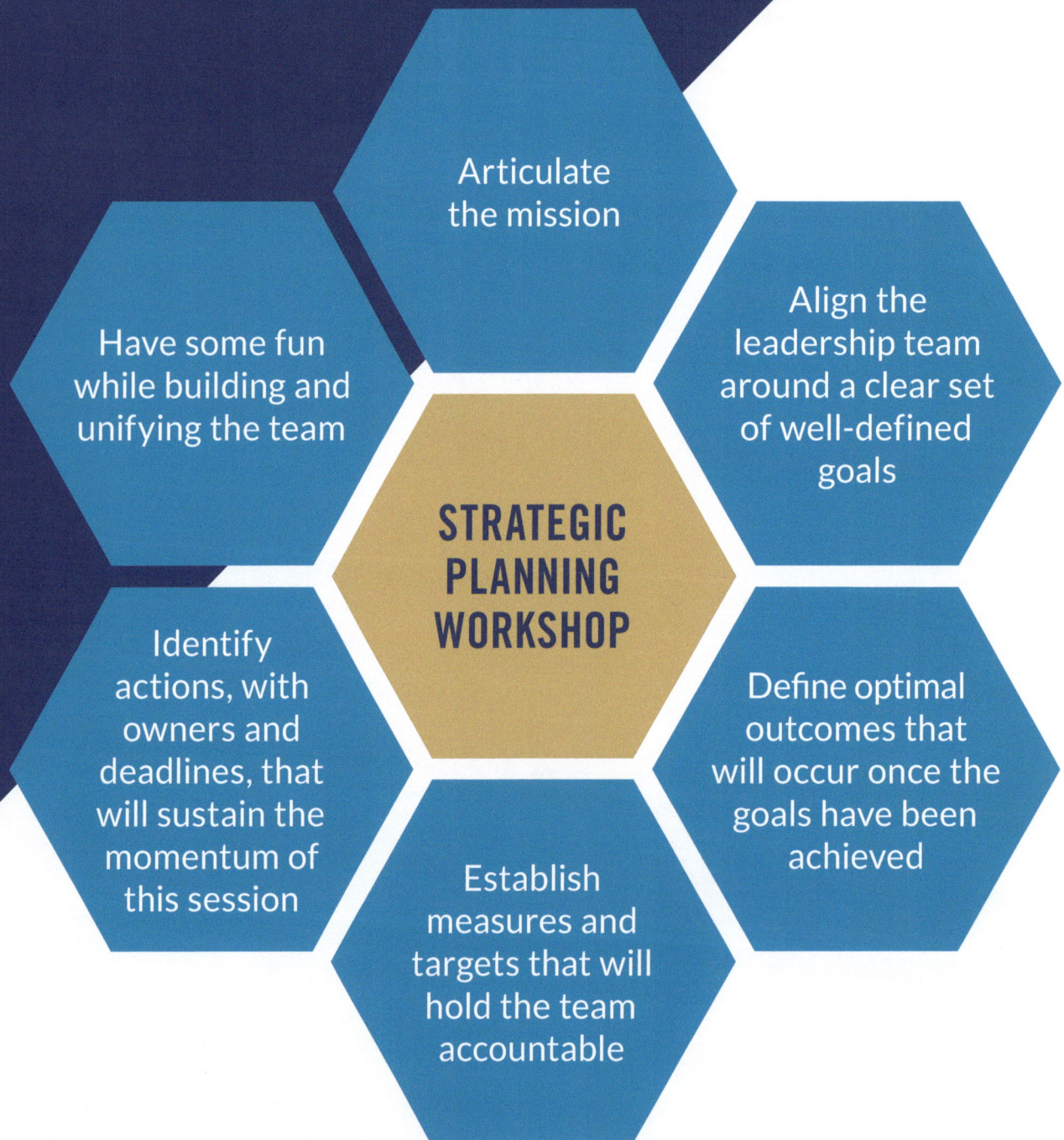

OBJECTIVES

Articulate the mission

Align the leadership team around a clear set of well-defined goals

Have some fun while building and unifying the team

STRATEGIC PLANNING WORKSHOP

Define optimal outcomes that will occur once the goals have been achieved

Identify actions, with owners and deadlines, that will sustain the momentum of this session

Establish measures and targets that will hold the team accountable

DEAR READER,

Here's my promise to you: this workbook won't waste your time! The process and approaches you're about to be introduced to have been road-tested by people as discerning, smart, and impatient as you! You want stuff that works now, and you've come to the right place.

It may sound a little cocky to so confidently and definitively assert that these materials work. It might help to know that I couldn't always proclaim that with the same degree of confidence. It is by doing a lot of less-than-perfect strategic planning engagements that the process steps got refined and enhanced. **You've got to get a few things wrong before you can get a lot of things right.**

It may also help to know where the framework, processes, and methods of this program got road-tested. In addition to countless corporate and nonprofit clients, my company, **Giant Leap Consulting,** has conducted strategic planning engagements for scientific research centers at Harvard, MIT, Brown, Yale, UPenn, Cornell, UMass, GA Tech, NC State, Purdue, Michigan State, USC, and the University of Colorado, to name a few.

Like you, scientists have a high need for tools and approaches that help them accurately **assess, manage, and, hopefully, control the future.** One of my company's proudest testimonials came from a researcher at MIT who, after setting a strategic plan using our process, said, "It wasn't the bullshit I was expecting."

A full-on strategic planning consulting engagement can be an expensive proposition. I believe that the investment in an organization's future far outweigh the expense of going through a strategic planning process. I also recognize, however, that some organizations—such as nonprofits or governmental agencies—are often hamstrung with budget limitations that leave them with the choice of not doing strategic planning at all, or doing it poorly. For these organizations a doing-it-yourself approach is the only viable option. The good news is, **this workbook will help you develop a rock-solid strategic plan for your organization.**

Here's to a bright future for you and the organization you serve!

Bill Treasurer

BILL TREASURER
Founder, Giant Leap Consulting, Inc.
(GiantLeapConsulting.com)

"

EFFORTS

AND

COURAGE

ARE NOT ENOUGH

WITHOUT

PURPOSE

AND

DIRECTION."

— JOHN F. KENNEDY
35th president of the United States

STRATEGIC PLANNING

DEFINITION:

A collaborative process whereby an organization clarifies its direction by developing its mission, top-level goals, objectives and measures, actionable strategies, and process for monitoring the plan.

THE FOUR MAJOR QUESTIONS THAT THE STRATEGIC PLAN SERVES TO ANSWER ARE:

1. Where are we today?

2. Where do we want to be tomorrow?

3. How will we close the gap?

4. What will we do to monitor our progress?

"**Plans are worthless. Planning is everything.**"
—*Dwight D. Eisenhower*

Ideally, the strategic plan should be used to drive decisions, actions, and even behaviors throughout the enterprise. The plan should "cascade" downward.

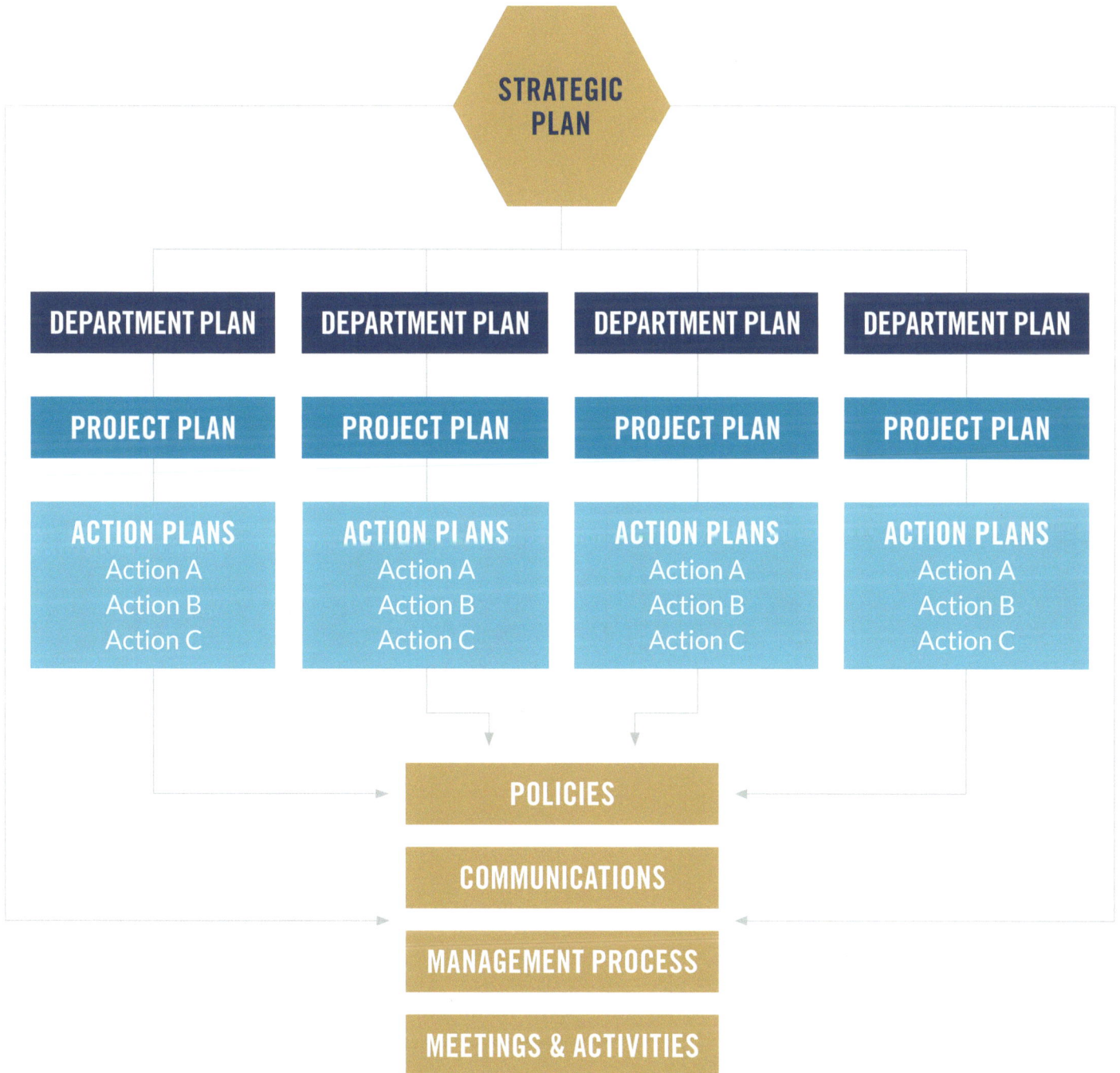

STRATEGIC PLAN

DEPARTMENT PLAN	DEPARTMENT PLAN	DEPARTMENT PLAN	DEPARTMENT PLAN
PROJECT PLAN	PROJECT PLAN	PROJECT PLAN	PROJECT PLAN
ACTION PLANS Action A Action B Action C	ACTION PLANS Action A Action B Action C	ACTION PLANS Action A Action B Action C	ACTION PLANS Action A Action B Action C

POLICIES

COMMUNICATIONS

MANAGEMENT PROCESS

MEETINGS & ACTIVITIES

PLAN THE WORK, THEN WORK THE PLAN!

STAKEHOLDER ASSESSMENTS

DEFINITION:
A stakeholder is any group or organization that has an interest in the organization's work or is affected by its work. Stakeholders have a "stake" in the organization's work.

A STRATEGIC PLAN PROCESS should start by identifying all the "stakeholders" who have a vested interest in the success of your organization.

EXTERNAL STAKEHOLDERS

INTERNAL STAKEHOLDERS

1. Who are the external stakeholders who are impacted by your success?

2. Who are the internal stakeholders who are impacted by your success?

MISSION

Overarching statement of your organization's "charge" and the challenge that directs its work.

GOAL AREAS

G O A L S

Top-level focus areas that collectively represent the overall mission's piece-parts.

OPTIMAL OUTCOMES

Ideal conditions that could emerge if a given goal area were being significantly advanced.

UNITS OF MEASURE

Metrics that can be tracked and monitored to gauge progress toward a given desired outcome.

SMART TARGETS

Specific long-term, mid-term, and near-term objectives to assess goal progress and motivate employees.

ACTION ITEMS

Finite and mission-critical actions that will advance desired outcomes and goals.

MISSION STATEMENT

DEFINITION:

A statement of direction that is brief, flexible, and distinctive. A mission should express an organization's reason for being. It should answer what you do, who you do it for, and the benefits that may be derived from your work.

Forbes
To deliver information on the people, ideas and technologies changing the world to our community of affluent business decision makers.

Southwest
Dedication to the highest quality of Customer Service delivered with a sense of warmth, friendliness, individual pride, and Company Spirit.

amazon.com
To be Earth's most customer-centric company, where customers can find and discover anything they might want to buy online, and endeavors to offer its customers the lowest possible prices.

Coca-Cola
To refresh the world... To inspire moments of optimism and happiness... To create value and make a difference.

f
To give people the power to share and make the world more open and connected.

Microsoft
To empower every person and every organization on the planet to achieve more

Starbucks
To inspire and nurture the human spirit—one person, one cup and one neighborhood at a time.

The Walt Disney Company
Using our portfolio of brands to differentiate our content, services and consumer products, we seek to develop the most creative, innovative and profitable entertainment experiences and related products in the world.

IDENTIFYING YOUR MISSION

Working with your team, answer the questions below:

WHAT DOES THIS ORGANIZATION DO?

WHO DOES THIS ORGANIZATION DO IT FOR?

HOW DO THEY BENEFIT?

10

DRAFT YOUR MISSION

DRAWING ON SOME OF THE WORDS, THEMES, AND PHRASES FROM THE QUESTIONS YOU JUST ANSWERED, WORK WITH YOUR GROUP TO DRAFT A MISSION STATEMENT.

QUALITY CHECK:

- Does the Mission describe your reason for existing?
- Does it indicate the audience served and how they benefit?
- Does it distinguish and differentiate you from others?
- Will the Mission motivate your team members?
- Will the mission inspire others to take an interest in your organization?

GOAL STATEMENT

DEFINITION:
High-level imperatives, long-term in nature, when accomplished collectively signal the achievement of the mission.

Before defining the Goal Statement, first decide on a limited set of HIGH-LEVEL GOAL AREAS that the mission must satisfy. Goal Areas can be thought of as the critical piece-parts upon which the mission is built. Some examples of Goal Areas and their associated Goal Statements from various Giant Leap clients are provided below.

MANAGEMENT

We successfully operate as a high-functioning organization that respects the contributions of the team, rises to the demands of the work, and is an enjoyable environment for all.

PROGRAM DEVELOPMENT

Execute high-quality, sustainable, and integrated programs that meet the needs of multiple customer bases while maintaining a consistent system of policies and procedures.

OUTREACH AND COMMUNICATION

Employ a targeted communication strategy that shares information on research outcomes to stakeholders in order to promote greater understanding and awareness of the project in our state.

FINANCIAL

A sustainable and transparent financial management system is in place to support the work and opportunities of the organization.

TECHNOLOGY

Provide a best in class technology portal/solution that is scalable, flexible, and easy to use.

DRAFTING YOUR GOAL STATEMENTS

GOAL AREA:

GOAL STATEMENT:

GOAL AREA:

GOAL STATEMENT:

GOAL AREA:

GOAL STATEMENT:

GOAL AREA:

GOAL STATEMENT:

GOAL AREA:

GOAL STATEMENT:

OPTIMAL OUTCOMES

DEFINITION:

Optimal outcomes are the conditions that one would expect to see if the Goal Statement were being actualized. A given Goal, when being significantly advanced, will likely produce multiple Optimal Outcomes. Optimal Outcomes can be thought of as the differences that will be made when the progress toward Goal attainment is significant.

Generally, a team will have up to **5 OPTIMAL OUTCOMES** per Goal Area. An example of an Optimal Outcome might be: *When the Customer Goal is being significantly advanced, optimally, an organization's customers are recommending their services to other potential clients.* Other Optimal Outcome examples from Giant Leap clients are offered below.

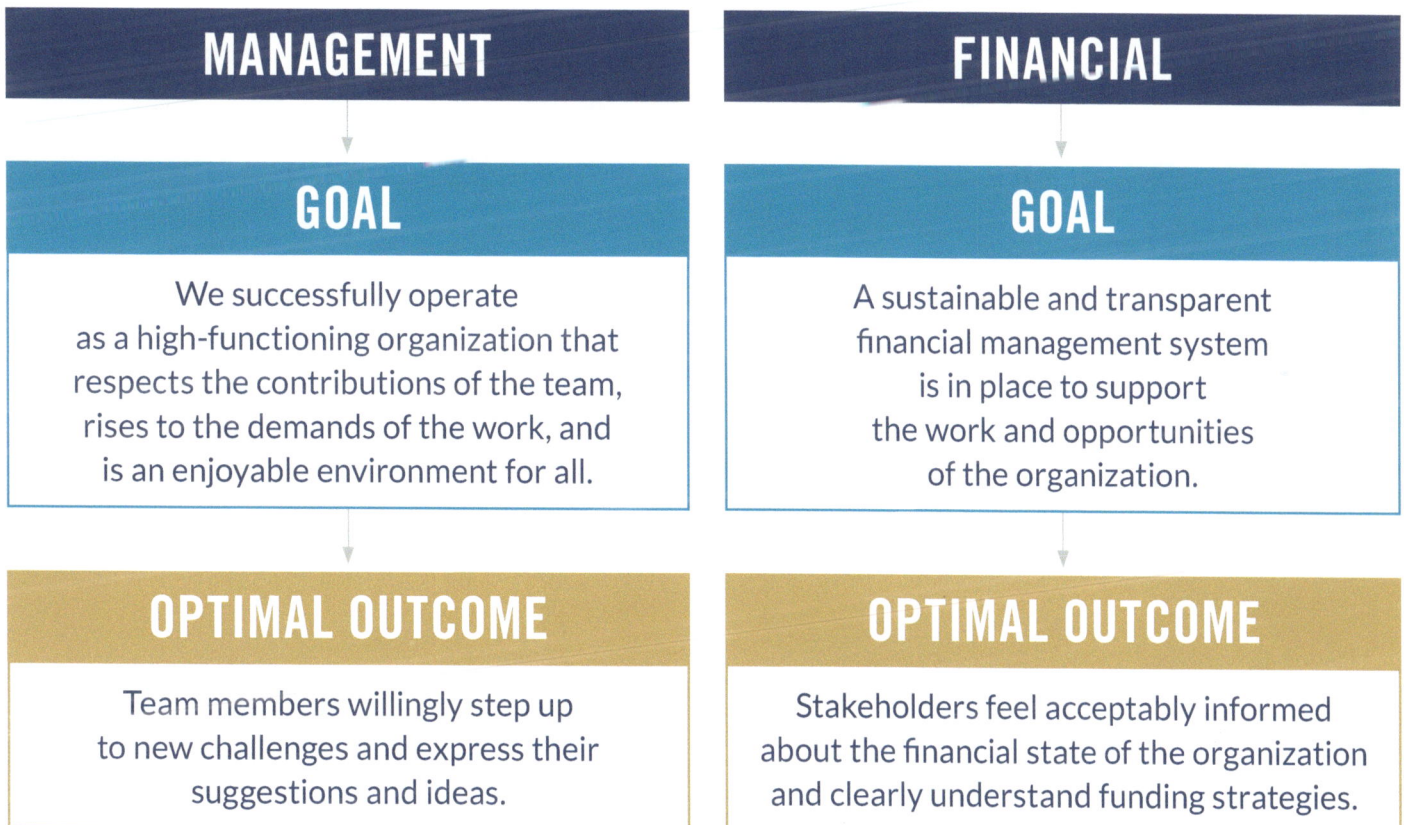

MANAGEMENT

GOAL

We successfully operate as a high-functioning organization that respects the contributions of the team, rises to the demands of the work, and is an enjoyable environment for all.

OPTIMAL OUTCOME

Team members willingly step up to new challenges and express their suggestions and ideas.

FINANCIAL

GOAL

A sustainable and transparent financial management system is in place to support the work and opportunities of the organization.

OPTIMAL OUTCOME

Stakeholders feel acceptably informed about the financial state of the organization and clearly understand funding strategies.

DRAFTING YOUR OPTIMAL OUTCOMES

When envisioning and defining Optimal Outcomes, state them as if they've already been achieved. For example, use words like "WE HAVE" and "WE ARE," not "We will" or "We plan to." Optimal Outcomes are identified by taking each Goal Statement and asking, "If this goal were being significantly advanced, what outcomes, optimally, would we expect to see?"

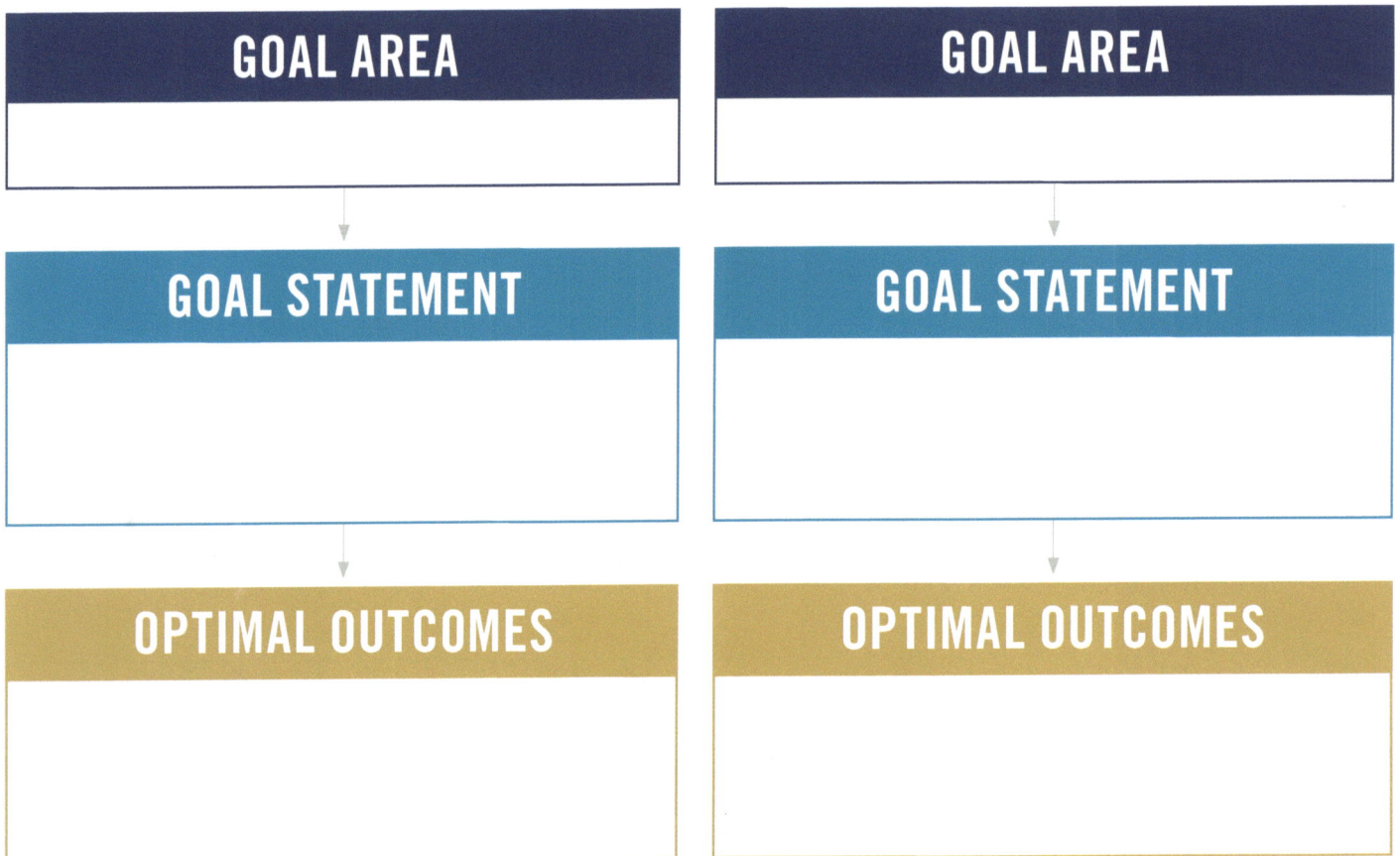

GOAL AREA	GOAL AREA

GOAL STATEMENT	GOAL STATEMENT

OPTIMAL OUTCOMES	OPTIMAL OUTCOMES

QUALITY CHECK:

- Are the outcomes stated as if they've already occurred?
- Is the outcome something that is truly likely to occur if the goal is being significantly advanced?

UNITS OF MEASURE

DEFINITION:

A metric that can be used to measure whether progress is being made on Goals and/or Optimal Outcomes. Often refers to the "number of" or "percent of." Units of Measure can be thought of as the yardstick on which organization goals will be tracked.

By identifying your Units of Measure carefully, you are preparing the way to **EFFECTIVELY SET YOUR SMART TARGETS.** Units of Measure are the yardsticks you will use to measure your effectiveness. Another way to consider it, your Unit of Measure is **THE ROAD YOU WANT TO GO DOWN.** Your SMART Target is the destination at which you want to eventually arrive. The first step to getting there is picking the road, or the Unit of Measure, that is most appropriate for your organization.

UNITS OF MEASURE EXAMPLES:

PUBLIC AWARENESS UNIT OF MEASURE:
Number of requests for presentations and training sessions.

FINANCIAL UNIT OF MEASURE:
Amount of reserved funds.

LEADERSHIP & MANAGEMENT UNIT OF MEASURE:
Number of cross-department initiatives.

DRAFTING UNITS OF MEASURE

GOAL #1 UNITS OF MEASURE:

GOAL #2 UNITS OF MEASURE:

GOAL #3 UNITS OF MEASURE:

GOAL #4 UNITS OF MEASURE:

GOAL #5 UNITS OF MEASURE:

QUALITY CHECK:

- Are you focusing on results?
- Do they include short and long-term measures?
- Are they areas that you can have control or great influence over?

SMART TARGETS

Specific, Measurable, Actionable, Realistic and Time-bound
targets that measure the progress toward goal attainment.

- Measures can be thought of as the exact location on the yardstick for each goal area.
- Short-term, mid-term, and long-term SMART Targets should be identified.

Remember, the goal is the outcome you want to achieve. The measures are how you will get there. When determining your measures and targets, it can be helpful to ask, "HOW WILL WE KNOW WHEN THIS GOAL IS ACHIEVED?"

NOTE: MEASURE RESULTS, NOT ACTIVITIES.

👎 POOR: The number of QA audits conducted

👍 GOOD: Average number of defects down to 1 per 6,000,000

GOAL

Increase financial reserves to enhance the organization's sustainability and provide a cushion during challenging economic environments

UNIT OF MEASURE	BASELINE	YEAR 2 TARGET	YEAR 3 TARGET
Reserved funds (financial reserves)	Establish year 1 base-line	Increase financial reserves by 10% over baseline by the end of year two	Increase financial reserves by 15% over year two actuals by the end of year three

SMART TARGETS

Targets the exact location on the Unit of Measure that was selected to gauge progress toward the Optimal Outcomes associated with a major Goal.

Once the Goals are defined, each Goal should be "drilled down" with specific Units of Measure and SMART TARGETS. Units of Measure can be thought of as the "yardstick", and the SMART TARGETS can be thought of as the exact location on the yardstick for each Goal area. Both short-term and long-term Measures/Targets should be defined.

NOTE: MEASURE RESULTS, NOT ACTIVITIES.
SPECIFIC | MEASURABLE | ACTIONABLE | REALISTIC | TIME-BOUND

EXAMPLE: WORKPLACE MORAL

GOAL

Design and nurture a positive work environment where staff and volunteers are valued and respected, have opportunities to develop new skills, and are recognized for their contributions to the mission.

OPTIMAL OUTCOME

An established, continuing education and development program for staff affiliated with local universities.

UNIT OF MEASURE

Number of staff continuing their education through local universities.

SMART TARGET

Increase number of staff enrolled in continuing education opportunities by 10% by end of Q3.

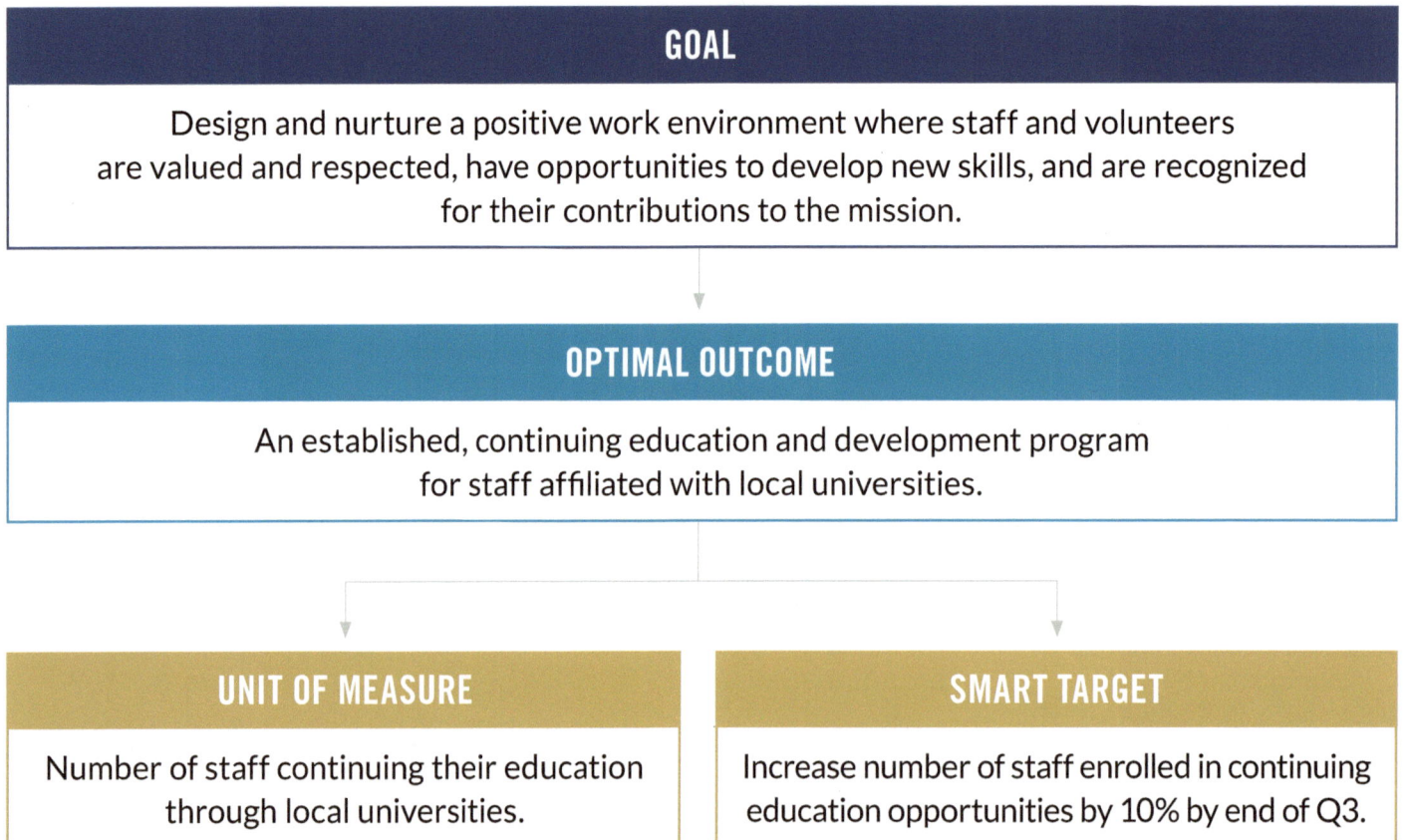

EXAMPLES:

SAFETY

- **50% reduction of number of injuries/accidents** based on the average of the last three years by the end of the next fiscal year.
- **50% reduction of number of lost work days** based on the average of the last three years by the end of the next fiscal year.

FINANCIAL

- 50% of all jobs will have a **35% or greater gross profit margin** at the close of this year.
- **Increase the amount of private market work** our company does by 20% of base business by the end of this year.
- Increase our **base business by 25%,** and **total business by 71%,** by the end of this year.
- **Increase cash reserves by 20%** by the end of this current fiscal year.
- **Reduce account receivables** time by 5 calendar days by the end of this year.

EMPLOYEE SATISFACTION AND MORALE

- **Increase employee satisfaction** by 15% as measured by our annual employee satisfaction survey.
- **Increase year over year retention** of current employees by 10% annually.
- **Reduce employee turnover** by 10% by the end of the current year.

CUSTOMER SERVICE

- Have **zero warranty call-backs** by the end of the current year.
- **Increase unsolicited customer testimonials** by 25% by the end of the current year.
- **Increase sales of new products to current customers** by 15% by the end of the fiscal year.
- **Increase sales of existing products to current customers** by 10% by the end of the fiscal year.
- **Reduce customer complaints** by 25% by the end of this year.
- **Increase customer satisfaction** by 15% as measured by our annual customer satisfaction survey.

	SHORT-TERM TARGETS	MID-TERM TARGETS	LONG-TERM TARGETS
1			
2			
3			
4			
5			

QUALITY CHECK:

- Are the Targets **S M A R T**? (**S**pecific, **M**easurable, **A**ctionable, **R**ealistic and **T**ime-bound)
- Are you measuring RESULTS, not activities?
- Are they stated in terms of increase, reduce, maintain, etc.?
- If all the Targets are achieved, will the Goal be attained?

ACTION ITEMS

DEFINITION:
Specific tasks, or actions, that need to be accomplished in order to meet your Goals and Optimal Outcomes.

To accomplish your Goals, work must be done, work that is being added to already full plates. To help prioritize, it's important to map out the critical actions that will **MOVE THE TEAM TOWARD THE ACHIEVEMENT OF OPTIMAL OUTCOMES.**

Replicate copies of the template below. Drawing on the Optimal Outcomes identified earlier, complete one template per critical action that needs to be taken to advance the critical action.

GOAL AREA:

OPTIMAL OUTCOME:

ACTION ITEM:

ACTION OVERSEER:

DUE DATE:

STAYING POWER THROUGH GOAL SETTING

Most people perform better when they are heading toward a goal. As such, it is important that everyone has a few key goals that they are responsible for achieving. Of course your individual goals should connect to the goals of your team as well.

WHEN SETTING GOALS, CONSIDER USING A "GOAL LADDER" LIKE THE ONE BELOW:

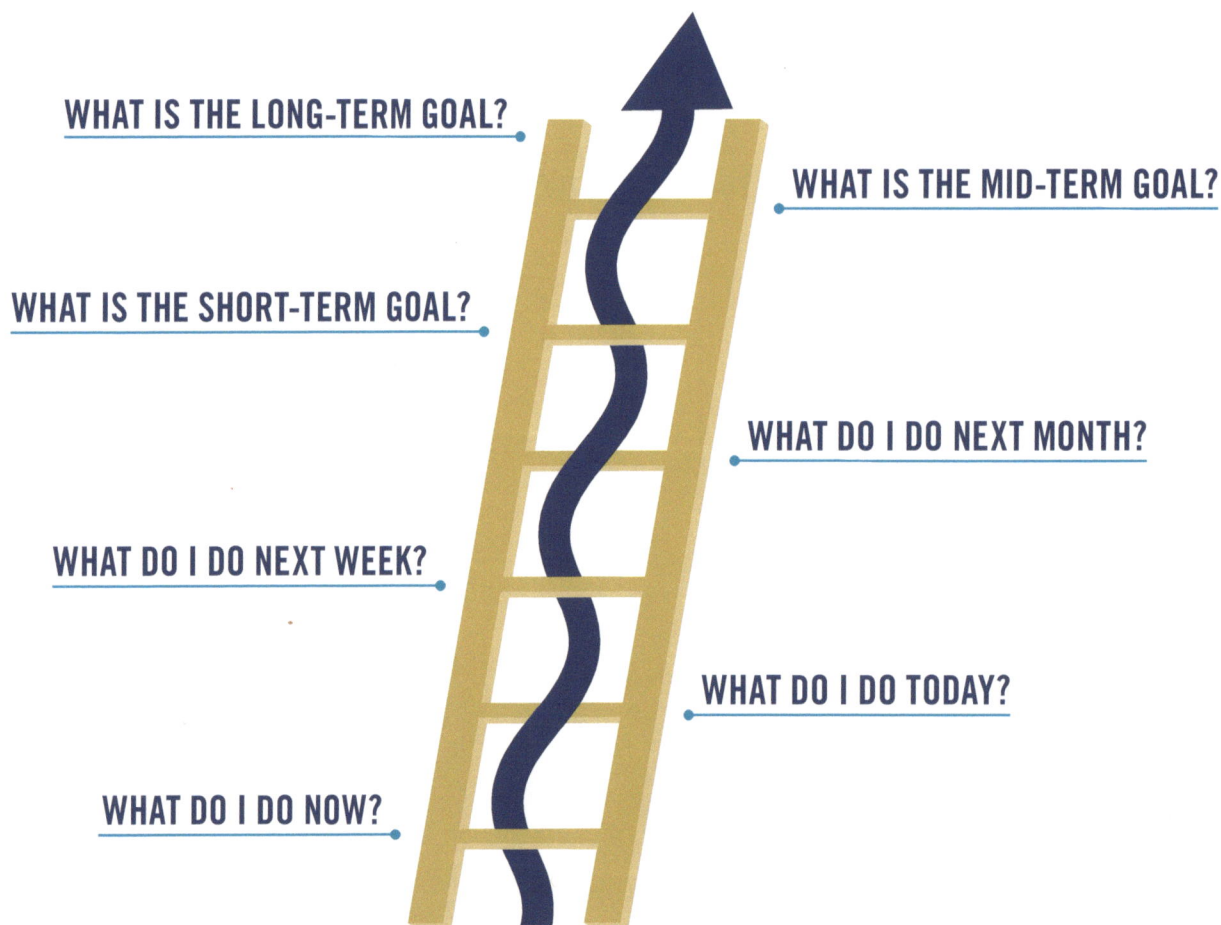

WHAT IS THE LONG-TERM GOAL?

WHAT IS THE MID-TERM GOAL?

WHAT IS THE SHORT-TERM GOAL?

WHAT DO I DO NEXT MONTH?

WHAT DO I DO NEXT WEEK?

WHAT DO I DO TODAY?

WHAT DO I DO NOW?

"Far and away the best prize that life has to offer is the chance to work hard at work worth doing."
—Theodore Roosevelt

STRATEGIC EXECUTION

Congratulations for drafting all the essential elements of a rock-solid strategic plan! Having a great plan is the surest way to create a successful future! Now, however, the REAL work begins: EXECUTION!

REMEMBER, SUCCESSFUL STRATEGIC EXECUTION TAKES:

- **Aggressive leadership** and **organized management**
- Continuous **monitoring, evaluating,** and **re-strategizing**
- Enterprise-wide personal **accountability**
- Many **owners, champions,** and **sponsors**
- Real **consequences** and **rewards**
- **COURAGE!**

AS YOU MOVE FORWARD WITH YOUR IMPLEMENTATION, BE SURE TO...

- Relentlessly **communicate** the strategy to all stakeholders.
- Drive operational improvement, but to **serve the strategy** (not BE the strategy).
- **Maintain discipline** in the face of many emergencies, interruptions, and distractions.
- **Measure progress** against the strategy using appropriate metrics.
- Nurture a **CULTURE that advances the strategy.**

NEED GUIDANCE OR COACHING ON YOUR PLAN? OUR TEAM IS STANDING BY!
info@giantleapconsulting.com.

GOOD STRATEGY QUESTIONS

The framework you completed to build your strategic plan should be considered basic but sound. You covered the essentials. To add DIMENSION AND DEPTH to your plan, we offer these additional Good Strategy Questions for your consideration. After answering them, you may wish to go back and revise and enhance your plan. Remember, planning takes planning, and more planning!

CUSTOMER QUESTIONS

- What are the ways we describe ourselves to our customers that might no longer apply?

- What would critical customers say about us? Any truth to those views?

- What is our brand, and how do we best articulate it to the marketplace?

- How will our strategic plan impact our ability to serve our clients? How will it impact our relationships with clients?

- If more of our book of business will be determined by relationships, how do we build those kinds of relationships?

- If a good customer were to leave, what would most likely be the reason?

GENERAL STRATEGY QUESTIONS

- What do we have/do that is truly strategic? (distinguishes us from our competition)

- What industry changes would make our products/services obsolete?

- In what areas does it appear we are pursuing "distractions disguised as opportunities?"

- Where is the company most vulnerable?

- What do you see as the major strategic challenges facing the business in the next 5 years?

- What are the likely consequences if we don't effectively respond to the challenges you listed?

- What are the truly important measures of strategic performance?

- If a competitor wanted to put us out of business, how would they go about doing it?

- What is something you have seen one of our competitors doing that we should be doing?

IMPROVEMENT OPPORTUNITIES

- What are the next areas of technological innovation we should pursue?

- Are there things that we do that don't make sense to you? Why do you think we do them?

- Are there areas in which we say one thing but do another?

PEOPLE/TALENT MANAGEMENT

- What employee training/development programs need to be added or improved?

- How can we do a better job of recruiting at senior levels without resorting to headhunters?

- How do we preserve our organization's culture in light of our recent changes (e.g., geographic expansion, new acquisitions, reductions in force, etc.)?

- What skills and behaviors are rewarded in the firm? Who gets ahead here?

- What skills and knowledge need to be acquired to further the company's strategic goals?

- What motivates or drives people within the firm?

- Which groups are the most powerful within the firm and why?

- What behaviors will get you into trouble with management?

- Relative to managing the company's talent, what measures are most important?

"Your most unhappy customers are your greatest source of learning."
—Bill Gates

"

WE CHOOSE TO GO TO THE MOON.

WE CHOOSE TO GO TO THE MOON
IN THIS DECADE
AND DO THE OTHER THINGS,
NOT BECAUSE THEY ARE EASY,
BUT BECAUSE THEY ARE HARD,
BECAUSE THAT GOAL WILL SERVE
TO ORGANIZE AND MEASURE
THE BEST OF OUR ENERGIES AND SKILLS,
BECAUSE THAT CHALLENGE IS ONE
THAT WE ARE WILLING TO ACCEPT,
ONE WE ARE UNWILLING TO POSTPONE,
AND ONE WHICH WE INTEND TO WIN."

— JOHN F. KENNEDY
Launching NASA's space program, September 12, 1962

STRATEGIC PLANNING GLOSSARY OF TERMS

ACTIONS: Specific tasks that are assigned to specific individuals or groups of individuals. Each action should connect to an objective or multiple objectives, and should link to the overall purpose. Actions that do not link to the purpose are distractions from it.

GOALS: Overarching aims that stem from the mission, and clarify where you will concentrate your resources and energies. Goals should be few in number. If you have more than five, you probably have too many. When all the goals have been achieved, the mission has been accomplished.

MISSION: The mission should define what the organization is trying to achieve. It defines the purpose, its "reason for being", and what it hopes to achieve. The mission directs the work in the here and now, and helps inspire people to work hard to reach a desired future state. A mission should be inspiring, meaningful, and pursuing something right. It does not define how you will operate, but simply why. It is helpful to think of your mission as what you want to be remembered for once the work is done.

OPTIMAL OUTCOMES: Optimal Outcomes are the conditions that one would expect to see if the Goal Statement were being actualized. A given Goal, when being significantly advanced, will likely produce multiple Optimal Outcomes. Optimal Outcomes can be thought of as the differences that will be made when the progress toward Goal attainment is significant.

SMART TARGETS: Specific, measurable, actionable, realistic, and time-bound targets that specify the exact location on the Unit of Measure that was selected to gauge progress toward the Optimal Outcomes associated with a major Goal. SMART Targets provide specific measures for assessing the impact of the work, and gauging whether it is advancing towards its goals. Measuring targets helps assess whether resources are allocated optimally to produce results. Measurable targets help you monitor progress; identify which programs are having the most impact, and which are not. Targets are related to, but more granular than goals. Targets are measurable aims for accomplishing the goals, and, unlike goals, are always attached to a deadline and/or timeframe.

STAKEHOLDERS: Stakeholders can be thought of as the people who will derive benefit and value from your work. It includes the people, inside or outside of the organization, whose lives may be changed by your work. Some organizations refer to stakeholders as "customers" or "clients".

STRATEGIC PLAN: The overall framework that organizes the organization's work, and encompasses the mission, goals, objectives, measures, and action steps. The plan defines where you want to be, and how you intend to get there. Strategic plans are practical and action-oriented, and involve setting targets, defining responsibilities, and making decisions about where you will take risks. The strategic plan begins with the purpose and ends with action steps.

UNITS OF MEASURE: The yardstick used to measure progress made in toward an Optimal Outcome. The Unit of Measure is the first element of identifying SMART Targets.

VISION: A statement that creates an image of the organization's desired future state. It is different from a mission in that a mission focuses on an organization's "charge", and a vision focuses on what the organization will look like when the mission is accomplished. Typically a vision is inspirational, lofty, and idealistic.

NOTES

DEAR CLIENTS AND FRIENDS,

You are the focus of everything we do at Giant Leap Consulting. When you leave a Giant Leap workshop, seminar or keynote, you will be armed with practical strategies and tools that you can immediately put to use back at work. As I often tell our clients, the person leaving our training programs should not be the same person who entered it. You deserve to be more confident, skilled and capable after experiencing a Giant Leap program.

Since our founding in 2002, Giant Leap has been fortunate to have worked with thousands of executives from some of the best organizations in the world. You've taught us a lot about what works—and what doesn't—when it comes to adult learners. You can count on us to always provide learning experiences that have rich content, insightful dialogue, engaging activities, and relevant case studies.

There's something else you can count on too: first-rate course materials. Our participant notebooks, PowerPoints, and course materials are among the best in the world. I know that's a tall claim, but it's true! You can sample our course material and see for yourself!—just send an email to info@giantleapconsulting.com.

Please take a moment to immerse yourself in Giant Leap's new course catalogue. In addition to introducing our tried-and-true training courses, it also showcases our two "signature" programs: Courageous Leadership, and Open-door Leadership.

Stay Courageous!

Bill Treasurer

BILL TREASURER
Founder, Giant Leap Consulting, Inc.
(GiantLeapConsulting.com)

P.S. Need a customized course? Giant Leap loves to develop new and original content for our clients!
Contact: info@giantleapconsulting.com

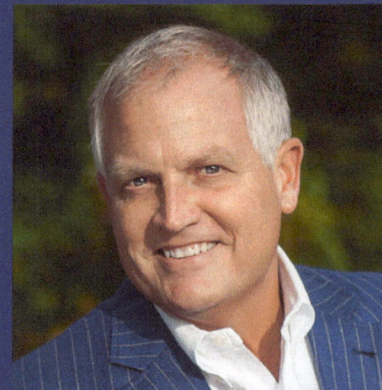

ABOUT BILL'S KEYNOTES

In the past two decades, thousands of executives across the globe have attended Bill's keynotes and workshops. Benefiting from the concepts first introduced in Bill's best-selling books, participants come away with stronger leadership skills, improved team performance, and more career backbone.

Among others, Bill has led workshops for NASA, Accenture, Lenovo, USB Bank, CNN, Hugo Boss, SPANX, the Centers for Disease Control and Prevention, the U.S. Department of Veterans Affairs, and the Pittsburgh Pirates.

Bill's insights about courage and risk-taking have been featured in over 100 newspapers and magazines, including the Washington Post, NY Daily News, Chicago Tribune, Atlanta Journal Constitution, Boston Herald, Woman's Day, Redbook, Fitness, and The Harvard Management Update.

VISIT OUR WEBSITES:
giantleapconsulting.com
billtreasurer.com

Little Leaps Press, Inc.
2 Lynwood Road
Asheville, NC 28804

Bulk Order Sales: Special discounts may be available for large quantity sales. For details, call: 800 867-7239.

Title: Do-it-Yourself Strategic Planning
Author: Bill Treasurer
Publication Date: June 1, 2019
Publisher: Little Leaps Press, Inc.

Published in the United States of America
by Little Leaps Press, Inc.
ISBN: 978-1-948058-18-6

LITTLE LEAPS
— PRESS —